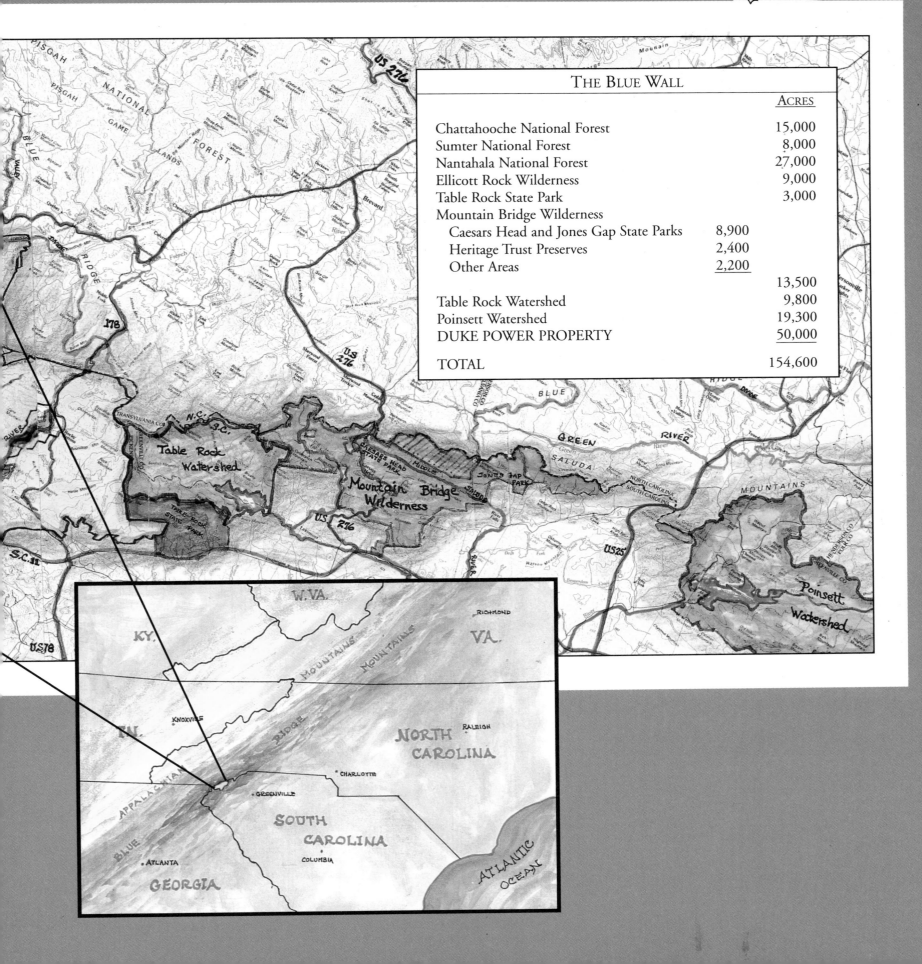

THE BLUE WALL

	ACRES
Chattahooche National Forest	15,000
Sumter National Forest	8,000
Nantahala National Forest	27,000
Ellicott Rock Wilderness	9,000
Table Rock State Park	3,000
Mountain Bridge Wilderness	

Caesars Head and Jones Gap State Parks	8,900	
Heritage Trust Preserves	2,400	
Other Areas	2,200	
		13,500
Table Rock Watershed		9,800
Poinsett Watershed		19,300
DUKE POWER PROPERTY		50,000
TOTAL		154,600

THE BLUE WALL

WILDERNESS OF THE CAROLINAS AND GEORGIA

PHOTOGRAPHY BY THOMAS WYCHE

TEXT BY JAMES KILGO

FOREWORD BY PAT NOONAN

WESTCLIFFE PUBLISHERS

SPONSORED BY
DUKE POWER COMPANY IN COOPERATION WITH
THE NATURE CONSERVANCY OF SOUTH CAROLINA

In Memory of

William States Lee III
1929-1996

*An engineer, environmentalist, and visionary—an active
and involved citizen of the Carolinas and of the world.*

Acknowledgments

The creation of this book, *The Blue Wall*, was an adventure and a challenge for both of us. The adventure came from exploring many parts of the Blue Ridge Escarpment we had never visited before. The challenge has been to convey in words and pictures the sights and feelings we experienced over the past year.

Duke Power Company, in cooperation with The Nature Conservancy of South Carolina, made this book possible. We are grateful for their generosity and support.

Duke Power Company has a worldwide reputation as the leader in power production, both nuclear and conventional, and has, for the last two decades, been the most efficient power producer in the country. Duke and its subsidiary, Crescent Resources, also have earned—and deserve—the reputation for wise management of their very large landholdings in this area and for encouraging active use of these lands by the public. Duke has received frequent national awards in recognition of these contributions.

Everyone at Duke and Crescent has been extremely helpful and cooperative in all parts of our explorations and studies. We particularly want to thank John Garton for his help in so many ways, from showing us an "invisible" green salamander in the crevice of a rock, to recounting the fascinating history of Lake Keowee and Lake Jocassee.

The Nature Conservancy, on the national level, naturally has an interest in the mountains and gorges which we depict in *The Blue Wall*. This property contains an exceptional variety of rare species of plants, a very diverse habitat environment for animals and plants, populations of Brook, Rainbow and Brown trout and good populations of a great variety of game. In short, this area is a biologist's dream!

The South Carolina chapter of The Nature Conservancy, under the direction of Patrick Morgan and his able staff, has already made a significant long-term impact on preserving large parts of the outstanding natural areas of South Carolina, ranging from the beaches and wetlands to the mountains. It could be a major and welcomed challenge over the next few years if they, along with other conservation organizations, could become involved in obtaining contributions and grants to protect the lands and gorges around Lake Jocassee.

—James Kilgo and Thomas Wyche

International Standard Book Number: 1-56579-189-4
Library of Congress Catalog Number: 96-60886
Photographs copyright Thomas Wyche, 1996. All rights reserved.
Text copyright James Kilgo, 1996. All rights reserved.
Foreword copyright Pat Noonan, 1996. All rights reserved.

Published by Westcliffe Publishers
2650 South Zuni Street
Englewood, Colorado 80110
Printed in Hong Kong by Palace Press International

Publisher, John Fielder
Production Manager, Patricia Coughlin
Designer, Amy Duenkel
Editor, Kiki Sayer
Proofreaders, Pat Shea, David Zimmerman

To receive a free color catalogue, call Westcliffe Publishers at 303-935-0900.

Frontispiece: The Toxaway River divides into two falls as it enters an endless deep gorge. Duke Power land, North Carolina.

Title page: The Blue Wall and white shafts of light stretch to the west. Caesars Head Park, Mountain Bridge Wilderness, South Carolina.

Opposite: Mountain Azalea. Sumter National Forest, South Carolina.

This book was made possible, in part, by special consideration given by the printer, Palace Press International.

FOREWORD

No place in the eastern United States is more ruggedly beautiful than the Blue Ridge Escarpment—the Blue Wall. Its hidden corners and dramatic scenery are captured affectionately in the pages of this magnificent volume. This craggy, rain-drenched land marks the fast-falling southern edge of the Appalachian Range, which stretches in majesty across South Carolina, North Carolina and Georgia. Here peregrine falcons soar, bears and bobcats roam, and turbulent rivers crash through rocky, laurel-lined gorges. A poet or painter can find inspiration on the shores of pristine Lake Jocassee, a 7,500 acre masterpiece, backed by mountains that rise almost 5,000 feet. A hiker can wander for miles past more towering waterfalls than any other place in the east. This is a land of mountains, waterfalls, and steep gorges.

Galax leaves encapsulated in winter ice. Caesars Head Park, Mountain Bridge Wilderness, South Carolina.

In the 150,000-acre heart of the Blue Wall, the rich variety of plants and animals, the clear lakes and streams, and the untouched mountains on the horizon are intact today thanks to the sound and cooperative management of public agencies, land trusts, private owners, and Duke Power Company and its subsidiary, Crescent Resources, Inc. Duke and Crescent own about 60,000 acres in the center of this spectacular wilderness. We are grateful to them for their intelligent and sensitive stewardship of this significant part of our mountain heritage. Over the decades this public-private cooperation has made the lands of the Blue Wall accessible to all in a way that protects their wildness and preserves their resources. We hope this exemplary partnership will continue to safeguard this rugged, beautiful and very special place.

The spirit-lifting book communicates the special wonder of the Blue Wall. The narrative by Jim Kilgo, a noted outdoor writer new to these mountains, takes us on a journey of discovery so vividly presented that we feel we are there with him as he struggles through rhododendron thickets or lands a trophy-sized trout. The brilliant photographs of Tommy Wyche, a long-time wanderer of the Escarpment, poignantly capture what makes this place so powerful—from its tiniest flowers to its mightiest peaks, from its bone-chilling flumes of whitewater to its calming canopies of hemlock, from its raging, boulder-strewn, cascading rivers to its placid high-country lakes.

The Blue Ridge Escarpment is one of America's treasures, a jewel of rare and irreplaceable worth. As a nation, it is our duty to safeguard these special places of wonder and beauty not just for today, but for the generations of Americans to come.

—Patrick F. Noonan, Chairman
The Conservation Fund

A reminder of a pioneer way of life; a grist mill on a small river. Oconee County, South Carolina.

PREFACE

The Jocassee Gorges comprise 60,000 acres of mountains, gorges and rivers surrounding a beautiful turquoise jewel—Lake Jocassee—7,500 acres of clear, cold, pure mountain water. This property, largely owned by Duke Power Company and its subsidiary, Crescent Resources, Inc., lies virtually in the center of 150,000 acres of the stunning Blue Ridge Escarpment, which stretches eastward from the west Fork of the Chattooga River in Georgia, some 60 miles into the Carolinas. Within this 150,00 acres

of unspoiled wilderness there are more than 50,000 acres of National Forest that lie to the west and north of the Jocassee Gorges. To the east, in South Carolina along the North Carolina state line, lie 40,000 acres of the Mountain Bridge Wilderness, a permanent nature preserve consisting of several state parks and two watersheds that supply drinking water for the Greenville, South Carolina area. The Jocassee segment, like the final "keystone" of a massive arch, joins together this 150,000-acre wild and undeveloped segment of the Blue Ridge Escarpment, aptly called "The Blue Wall" by the Cherokee Indians.

Consider that within this stretch of 30 miles of the Blue Wall are:

· Two of only four National Wild and Scenic Rivers in the southeastern United States, the Chattooga and the Horsepasture,

· Five deep gorges containing the racing waters of the Whitewater,

Fall on Lake Jocassee—cool water and warm autumn foliage. Duke Power land, South Carolina.

Thompson, Bearcamp, Horsepasture and Toxaway Rivers, as well as another smaller gorge containing the Eastatoe River and a South Carolina Heritage Trust Preserve,

· Some of the most spectacular waterfalls in the eastern United States: Windy Falls on the Horsepasture, the remote Thompson River Falls, Bearwallow and Bearcamp Creek Falls and Toxaway Creek Falls—perhaps the longest cascade of falls in the East,

· Ellicott's Rock Wilderness Area, a 9,000-acre National Wilderness on the Chattooga river at the joint boundary of Georgia and the Carolinas,

· Five South Carolina state parks: Devil's Fork (on the shores of Lake Jocassee), Oconee, Keowee-Toxaway, Jones Gap and Caesars Head,

· A massive expanse of forested peaks and river gorges comprising one of the largest and most varied headwater ecosystems in the eastern United States,

· An area varied enough in climate, orientation, altitude and soils to maintain an incredible variety of plant life, and

· Lake Jocassee, the turquoise jewel of the Blue Wall.

I have had the personal good fortune to have camped, hiked and floated for extended periods of time in some of the world's great wilderness areas. I have trekked in the Himalaya Mountains to Lake Tellicho—at 16,600 feet, the highest lake in the world; I have backpacked above the Arctic Circle in Alaska; paddled 225 miles down the Colorado River in the Grand Canyon; rafted the famed Tatshensheeni River in the Yukon; horse-backed in remote parts of Montana; canoed 320 miles from the Atlantic Ocean to the Gulf of Mexico across Florida's swamps and rivers; and skied and camped in the Sawtooth Mountains of Idaho. This is said with no sense of pride, but only to qualify my judgment that this portion of the Blue Ridge Escarpment in the Carolinas and Georgia—the Blue Wall—is truly one of the world's great wilderness areas.

It is impossible to communicate verbally just how spectacular these mountains, gorges, rivers and waterfalls are. Perhaps these photographs will help convey the beauty and excitement of the area. However, even photographs, no matter how breathtaking, cannot convey the feeling of being within the areas—either with friends or alone with the water, trees and rich terrain.

Jim Kilgo has done a masterful job of taking the reader through his exploration and first-time experiences of becoming acquainted with the area. I hope that Jim's writing and my pictures will give everyone a feeling of wonder, excitement and awe at such a "special place." It is not at all necessary to like hiking or camping or paddling to appreciate that this area is unique in so many different ways.

I hope this book will play a role in making people aware that this is a wilderness area of national significance, one of the world's great natural places—a place of "endless forest," sheer cliffs, foaming whitewater, trout, black bears and other wild mountain creatures. Beyond that, I hope this book encourages us—all of us—to actively support sound resource planning and management, and above all, permanent preservation of this and other "special places."

Those of us that live in this area are fortunate to have such a large unspoiled wilderness so close by. I feel very fortunate to have been able to capture on film some of the exceptional beauty within these mountains; the experience has heightened my appreciation of their splendor.

—Thomas Wyche

The Chattooga River, a National Wild River, comes of age near the North and South Carolina border. Nantahala National Forest, North Carolina.

The Gorges of the Blue Wall

by James Kilgo

I am no stranger to the highlands, but I go there as an outsider, a native of the coastal plain and a resident all my adult life of the Piedmont. For years I have hiked and camped and fished in north Georgia and a little in western North Carolina, but I had not known that section of the southeastern face of the Blue Ridge that stretches across the upper corner of my native South Carolina. I had hardly known of it. Growing up in Darlington, I thought the mountains were vaguely in the neighborhood of Asheville. When I moved to Athens, Georgia, 30 years ago, I headed north toward the country west of the Chattooga, failing again to take into account that wild, rugged borderland above Lake Jocassee. Now, at this rather advanced hour, when my stamina is not what it once was, I am eager to enter into those hills, to discover for myself how wild they are and by the tracks I make to stake my claim.

What it took to ignite that desire was a call from Tommy Wyche, the Greenville conservationist who founded Naturaland Trust and saved for us all the 40,000-acre natural area between Table Rock and Caesars Head known as the Mountain Bridge. Tommy told me about the gorges of the Blue Ridge Escarpment. He would take me up there, he said; he wanted me to write about what I found. The opportunity felt like a gift.

The gorges of the Blue Ridge Escarpment—what a beautifully sculpted phrase. Listen to it: you hear gouged, edged, cut, and carved, scooped, scoured, and scalloped. Say it aloud and you feel on your tongue and against your teeth and palate the rugged physical forms it designates. Those forms constitute a topography unlike any other I know. Within a 10-mile stretch, five gorges cut through the southeastern wall of the Blue Ridge—as though scored by the claws of a bear—from North Carolina down into South Carolina, converging toward Lake Jocassee. From west to east they are Whitewater, Thompson, Bear Camp Creek, Horsepasture, and Toxaway.

The circumstance that created the gorges was a slight shift in the eastern Continental Divide. For most of its length, from Georgia to Virginia, the divide follows the crest of the Escarpment, but for the 10-mile stretch above Lake Jocassee, it jogs to the north, creating between it and the crest a descending terrace that allows for the formation of watersheds. Rising on that terrace, the rivers acquire the volume it takes to cut deep into hard stone.

The Thompson River

November 26. It is autumn in the Georgia Piedmont, a little past the peak but many trees are still in color—scarlet oaks and dogwoods, maples all a-fire—from Athens up I-85 to the Cherokee Foothills Trail—S.C. 11—and on to Walhalla. But turn north beyond Walhalla and you climb quickly into winter. At 2,500 feet the trees are bare, the brown hillsides denuded, exposing their musculature, their bony rock. Winter here seems emp-

tier of life than it does at lower, flatter elevations, but each season has its compensations; in the mountains this time of year you can see. Pull off at a roadside overlook—there's a good one north of Whitewater Falls—and you get a view that leafier seasons don't afford. The five gorges and their dividing ridges lie before you, a frozen blue ocean—waves and troughs—as far as you can see. It's easy to believe that some Titan in the mythic past caught hold of this country by the edges and bunched it together like carpet. That, in fact, is about what happened.

In school I was taught that the Appalachians are old, worn down to gentle nubs and covered by vegetation, whereas the Rockies are young, dramatically high and craggy. I took that to mean that the western ranges were somehow more real, closer to God's idea of mountains. The poor old Appalachians—our mountains—were used up, no longer wild, home to people instead of grizzlies.

The differences between those two ranges cannot be explained, however, only by age. The Rockies are what geologists call Fault Block mountains, created by violent upheavals of broken sections—or blocks—of the earth's crust, whereas the Appalachians are Folded, land nudged together more gently into rhythmic ridges and valleys. Even so, these hills too stood jagged and rocky at first and remained so for a long, long time.

That event occurred during the Permian, 250 million years ago, an amount of time too vast for me to comprehend. But it helps to know that in those days there was only a single land mass—now called Pangaea—on the face of the earth, and the only animate life in that bleak, monotonous world were insects, amphibians, and a few small lizards. By the time of the great tectonic collisions that thrust up the Rockies, a mere 60 million years ago, Pangaea had long since come apart, and birds and mammals inhabited the earth. During the 190-million-year interval, wind-borne grit and ice-borne rock and running water had ground down, or subdued, the peaks in the east.

The geology of the southern Appalachians, however, does not explain why the southeastern edge of the mountains, instead of petering out in a series of diminishing

Thompson Falls cascades 300 feet to pool above Foothills Trail Bridge. Duke Power land, North Carolina.

ridges, as one might expect, drops off abruptly, falling 1,200 feet in about two miles. Theories have been published, but the cause interests me less than the event itself—the sudden, steep hill you climb when you turn north off S.C. 11. That hill is what the Cherokees called the Blue Wall.

I am riding with Tommy Wyche's daughter, Sally Coenen, winding our way up the face of the wall on our way to join her father. We meet him at the parking lot at Whitewater Falls. At this gray, chilly hour we have the place to ourselves. Tommy leads us up a blacktop path to the overlook, and there, across the chasm of the gorge, is the spectacle—a waterfall cascading white out of the evergreen forest, splashing down cliff face and terrace 600 feet to the floor below. Breathtaking, say the guidebooks. But somehow it doesn't take mine. Before me is a protective fence, its topmost rail polished to a high luster by the hands of thousands of sightseers. The falls has the feel of a thing that has been photographed too many times, and besides, I'm cranky enough not to want to be told by the state where I have to view it from.

The Foothills Trail passes through this overlook and from here descends into the gorge. Sally, who has been here before, leads me down 100 feet or so to another lookout, an outcrop of boulders unguarded by fence. We step up onto a rock. The shift in point of view has not been great enough to alter the appearance of the falls, but from here you feel removed from the crowd.

A strong wind is swirling through the gorge, driving a host of yellow leaves, the vestiges of autumn snatched and blown. The blue air between us and the long white cascade dances with yellow leaves.

Tommy has mentioned a waterfall on the Thompson River that he's been eager to photograph, but unlike Whitewater it's not accessible by road. To reach it, we'll have to walk in along the river three or four miles and then drop down into the gorge, descending like monkeys tree by tree. I'm not ready for that—recent elbow surgery—but at least we can walk in as far as the falls and see what it looks like from above.

I have been advised to bring my flyrod. I have never fished for trout this time of year, but why not? With the aluminum tube in one hand and felt-sole boots in my daypack, I follow Sally and her father down an old logging road closed to vehicular traffic. After 20 minutes we come upon the river. It crosses the road, not as wide or as deep as I had expected. Just as well because we are going to have to ford it. Sally and Tommy have brought knee-high rubber boots, but I plan to tough it across barefooted. The water is cold enough to hurt, but I am more concerned about staying upright on slick stone. Safely across and drying my reddened feet, I realize that without waders I can't fish. Accustomed to wading wet, I never stopped to realize that this is late November. Oh well. The rod's aluminum tube serves nicely as a staff.

The old road we're walking is mostly level. It follows the river. From time to time we come upon a blackened fire ring—an old fisherman's camp—but the woods are free of trash.

On our left the river has begun to fall. It is well below us now. To get down to it, we would have to scramble, catching hold of trees to break our momentum. In the road is a small cairn. Tommy wonders if that's a sign to other fisherman that this is a good place to descend. I doubt it, I say; trout fishermen keep their secrets to themselves.

Myriad fall leaves cling to a moist rock face. Jones Gap Park, Mountain Bridge Wilderness, South Carolina.

We have been hiking steadily for two hours through open hardwood forest, but I have seen only a chickadee and heard only two grouse flush.

Sally stops. "Listen," she says.

I can't hear from the left side but when I turn I catch the distant roar of falling water. Another hundred yards or so and it comes through loud and clear. The Thompson River Falls.

"That's big water down there," Sally says.

We try to see. Down through a terraced canopy of hemlock and pine and an understory of rhododendron I spy patches of white. Even the top of the waterfall is far below us, and it drops, Tommy says, another several hundred feet. Now that might take my breath, not because it's more dramatic than Whitewater—it couldn't be—but because it is hidden.

Sally says she's glad that there are still a few natural splendors that the world has not yet beaten a path to, and I'm reminded of how an object can be used up by too much seeing.

According to the trail guide, the falls can be approached from the bottom, but for that vantage point one has to hike in three and a half miles on the Foothills Trail and then, from the bridge over the river, rock-hop another mile upstream. Allow two hours from the bridge, the guide advises. Tommy and Sally have done that, but Tommy gained no point of view for his camera. He's determined to try the side of the gorge. But not today. It would be well after dark before we got back to the car.

December 4. Alone on the Foothills Trail, hiking from the trailhead at the Bad Creek Pumped Storage Station to the Thompson River, three and a half miles in. I'm not equipped to wade upstream to the falls today, not alone, but at least I can see the river.

According to the topo map, a great ridge angles southwest to northeast between the Whitewater and the Thompson. The trail will take me up the south face of the slope until it levels out on a contour near the top. From there it descends into the gorge.

The flank of the ridge is hardwood, a maturing forest bare of leaves, mostly white oak and hickory. At one time these hills were dominated by the American chestnut, a noble tree that was used by self-sufficient local residents for needs ranging from fences to furniture. But a blight, introduced in 1904, gradually destroyed the trees. Having never seen a mature chestnut, I cannot imagine an entire forest of them, but at this time of year they would have been just as bare as the oaks and hickories, the light as raw and glaring.

As I try to understand the mystery of mountains—the attraction they hold—it occurs to me that mountains are an alternative to the norm, which is the flat land where we build our cities and do our work. The mountains are where we go to get away. That habit started in the days before air conditioning, when the only relief from sweltering summer heat was in the highlands. But cool air alone does not explain the mystery. For me it has to do with a peculiar beauty, not so much of scenic splendor as of smaller things like grouse, trout, and trilliums that don't occur at lower elevations or beyond a narrow range of temperature. In the spring these hills will resound with the songs of warblers that don't nest in the flatlands, or I might hear at any moment the rumor of a distant waterfall. That I have to sweat to reach a place where these things can happen makes them that much more to be desired.

I'm sweating now, have tied my jacket around my waist.

Up ahead, beyond the shoulder of this hill, I see at last what could be the gorge of the Thompson River. Just as I think I hear a sound of water, I start down a steep set of steps toward the cool green shade of laurel and hemlock. And there below is the river—clear green water, smooth and fast, huge boulders, and a wooden bridge. Blue sky, reflected in the river, shines up in patches through dark foliage.

The bridge defines the scene, brings all elements into order. Connecting this side to over there, dividing upstream from down, it declares itself the center.

I walk out onto it. Below me on the downstream side lies a boulder as wide and flat as a banquet table. The stone is cool. I spread out my lunch—cheese and crackers, a sandwich, a tangerine—and give thanks, not for food alone but for the blessed flow of the river, the boulder, the blue sky, and solitude. A jet might pass overhead without my hearing it above the sound of rapids, and I have not seen a soul all day.

I may be in the neighborhood of a rare wildflower known to science as *Shortia galacifolia*, or by the lovely common name Oconee Bells. The botanist Andre Michaux discovered it somewhere hereabouts in 1787. It is a low-growing plant with glossy leaves, resembling galax. I've never seen it, but I resist an impulse to look around. More artist than botanist, I'd rather wait until it blooms.

With an annual rainfall of 80 to 90 inches, the Blue Wall is the wettest place in the eastern United States, and as a result, the flora of these mountains is one of the most richly diverse in the country. An extensive series of field studies sponsored by Highlands Biological Station during the 1960s documented the unique botanical features of the gorges. In the Horsepasture, for example, botanists have identified 580 species of vas-

cular plants. My interest in wildflowers is limited mostly to the showy species—orchids, iris, lilies and lady slippers—but the modest trilliums are my favorite. At least nine species grow in the mountain counties of North Carolina. All have three leaves (hence the name) but one group is sessile—the flowers standing upright—and the other is pedicillate, which means that the stalk of the flower—the pedicil—is bent so that the flower hangs face down beneath the leaves. The flowers of both types are either white, pale yellow, or one of several shades of maroon. None is bright and flamboyant. What I admire about them is their understated elegance. Finicky in their requirements, they don't sow themselves promiscuously on the wind, though when they find a place to their liking—a moist, shady glen—they may flourish in thick stands. I don't know which of the trilliums occur in these gorges, but I'm looking forward to April. I'd like to spend a weekend here with nothing to do but botanize.

A quick, darting movement out of the corner of my eye. Behind me, from a dark little crevice between the river bank and the boulder, a winter wren has appeared. For a moment he stands exposed on the naked stone, a brown bit of fluff almost as tiny as a hummingbird, and considers the intrusion I have made.

This little bird, as distinguished from his larger, more common cousin the Carolina wren, is a summer resident of the far north. Here along the rocky banks of the cold Thompson River he has found his winter playground. It is largely deserted, at least by birds, for most of the species that spent the spring and summer in these gorges had left for lands further south before the solitary winter wren arrived. I add him to my list of things to be thankful for. A December stream without at least one winter wren is bleak indeed.

Despite his presence, the mountains this time of year offer little attraction to the birdwatcher. Spring is the season for that. As devoid of birds as winter is, May in the mountains is vibrant with song and flight. The variety of species is greater here than at lower elevations. Species whose breeding range outside the mountains is further north nest in the southern Appalachians at elevations of 2,000 feet and higher. In other words, the birder who wants to hear a rose-breasted grosbeak singing on territory may, instead of driving to Pennsylvania, merely climb to 2,500 feet in North Carolina. There, as well, he

Campers enjoy a true wilderness perched just above Windy Falls. Horsepasture River, Duke Power land, North Carolina.

will find the scarlet tanager and a variety of warblers—the redstart, the chestnut-sided, the black-throated blue, and others that do not nest in the Piedmont. Like spring wildflowers, these shy but brightly colored birds will simply appear in the gorges some April night, and the person lucky enough to be here the next morning will hear them greet the sun in their various trills and buzzes.

According to Genesis 1, God created plants first, then fish, then birds, and finally mammals—a sequence no scientist can reasonably dispute. I am grateful for them all, but without the animals, the larger ones especially, the woods would still seem empty. Yet here, no matter the season, I do not expect to see even so much as a raccoon, certainly not at midday, much less the more secretive bobcats and foxes, weasels, skunks, and otters. They are around. You can prove their presence by the tracks they leave in

Abstract tree silhouette. Jones Gap Park, Mountain Bridge Wilderness, South Carolina.

the silt of old road beds. They just don't want to be seen.

If I am going to have to populate these mountains with a bestiary of my imagination, I might as well add to it some of the original inhabitants, like wolves and panthers. Long since extirpated, these animals left their tracks in the names of streams and gaps and balds scattered throughout the southern Appalachians, but I like to think that they are still out there, just outside the perimeter of empirical knowledge, like a feral dog beyond the light of a campfire.

It's that kind of wishful thinking that accounts for frequent reports of panthers. Our imagination seems to have relinquished the wolf to extinction, at least in the southeast, but panthers have held on, long past the last reliable evidence, apparently because of our need to believe in them.

It occurs to me that the animals I have mentioned are all predacious. Prey species—squirrels and deer, for example—are indeed more readily observed, but they lack the power to transform a natural area into wilderness. The fact that they appear regularly in suburban back yards is adequate proof of that. A definition of wilderness is finally up to the individual; for me it is an area sufficiently vast and remote to accommodate the range of a large predator. In the absence of wolves and panthers, bears will serve. Though not a predator, Ursus is a lordly presence with the power, as Indians knew, to enter into our dreams.

I'm speaking of the black bear. He is not a griz, to be sure. The possibility of his presence may not lift you to another level of feeling alive. But he has the advantage of living here, in the gorges of the Blue Ridge Escarpment, and as an answer to our need to know that we have entered the domain of a creature larger and more powerful than

ourselves, he will do quite well. To see a bear in the woods—even just to smell one or to come upon a place where a bear has slid down a hill ploughing a swath through jewelweed—is to feel the mountain move on its axis, to revert one phase back toward the way it used to be.

At midday on the Thompson River, the sun is warm enough to entice bears from their winter dens. As though my desire to see one might incarnate the images in my head, I turn to look downstream—and find myself face to face with two men. I jump. Fishermen have stolen upon me in the roar of the rapids. From the way they are dressed, I should probably call them anglers. I admire their neoprene waders, their complicated, many-pocketed vests, but not their rods. Decked out like an advertisement for a fly fishing magazine, they are casting with bait. Worms, it looks like.

One of the men—the designated talker—steps up onto my table. We observe the protocol of the stream, exchange greetings. If I keep my mouth shut, I'll learn more. And so I do. They are native North Carolinians who fish the Thompson often; it's a rough river to wade, but the fishing's good if you catch it right. They came in on a gravel road that begins at the Bad Creek parking lot. The road is open only during the deer season—not the best time to fish, but they take advantage of the opportunity, camping where the road crosses the river. Generally, they prefer fly fishing, but there ain't no point in it this time of year. A spawning brown won't hit nothing noway unless you just happen to drag your bait across him. Which is what they are hoping to do.

With that, my visitor moves on, hurrying to catch his silent partner. On my way out I stop on the bridge and watch them cast. They are headed toward the Thompson River Falls.

That's where I'm going one of these days when time and weather and the availability of any of several fishing buddies coincide. But it had better be soon. Once winter sets in, I'm afraid it will be too cold or too wet up here to camp. Then we'll have to wait for spring.

Whatever the weather between now and then, I will be back in April. The waterfall is a powerful attraction. So is the fishing, and maybe the river most of all. Looking upstream, I think it is the river. As it comes rushing down through the steep-sided gorge, I want to wade against its force, casting to deep green pools, until I hear above the rapids the roar of the falls and know by that sound that I have come about as far as I can. What I will find there are trilliums blooming in the mist and trout rising and the chance any moment that a bear might appear.

Blossoms of Silverbell tree on Chauga River. Sumter National Forest, South Carolina.

Lone pine bends to Winter's ice. Caesars Head, Mountain Bridge Wilderness, South Carolina.

Toxaway Creek Falls, one of the highest cascades in the East, flows into Lake Jocassee. Adjoining Duke Power land, North Carolina.

Previous page: Gold sunlight on Goldenrod field near Jones Gap Park, Mountain Bridge Wilderness, South Carolina.

Hearts-a-burstin'. Middle Saluda River, Jones Gap Park, Mountain Bridge Wilderness, South Carolina.

Mushrooms. Sumter National Forest, South Carolina.

Freshly minted leaves in the springtime. Caesars Head Park, Mountain Bridge Wilderness, South Carolina.

Lake Jocassee nestled in the mountains. Duke Power land, North Carolina.

Straight trees on steep sides of Whitewater River gorge at Foothills Trail bridge. Duke Power land, North Carolina.

A quietly moving mirror with a white ripple. Whitewater River, Nantahala National Forest, North Carolina.

A wasp's nest near Upper Whitewater Falls. Nantahala National Forest, North Carolina.

Bellwort. Chandler Heritage Preserve, Mountain Bridge Wilderness, South Carolina.

East Fork Overflow Creek drops precipitously to join the West Fork of the Chattooga River. Nantahala National Forest, North Carolina.

Indian Paintbrush. Ashmore Heritage Trust Preserve, Mountain Bridge Wilderness, South Carolina.

Sun rays feature mile upon mile of the Blue Ridge Escarpment. Caesars Head Park, Mountain Bridge Wilderness, South Carolina.

LAKE JOCASSEE

January 29. With Sally Coenen and my wife, Jane, on Lake Jocassee—a dreary day, light rain and temperature in the low 40s, but we are warm and dry in a covered pontoon boat. Our guide Jimmy Orr is giving us a tour of the upper end of the lake, heading north toward the wall where the rivers come in.

A boat on the open water is a good place for an unobstructed view of the Escarpment. It's not a wall, if by that you mean a flat vertical plane. What looms before us are mountains—ridges rising abruptly from the lake, their feet in the water. They rise quickly to an elevation of about 2,200 feet, 1,000 feet above the surface of Jocassee. And beyond the ridges that I can see on this dim morning are mountains another 1,000 feet higher—a broken, irregular wall, but a wall nonetheless. So it would have appeared to a traveller coming up from the south on horseback or afoot, before the age of automobiles. Whoa! How am I going to climb over that?

On the map before me, Jocassee looks like a crab with divided claws—the flooded channels of four rivers. Before the lake was built, the two rivers on the left—Whitewater and Thompson—came together as soon as they flowed out of their gorges, and on the right the Horsepasture and the Toxaway did the same. These two rivers, made of four, then met at the foot of Double Spring Mountain to form the beautiful Keowee.

They say it was beautiful, those who lived along its banks, but it's all under water now. When the Duke Power Dam was completed in 1973, the dancing green river stopped in its tracks, backed up to its waterfalls and overflowed them, and stilled the flow of its tributaries clear back to the gorges. And then the water level rose to meet the falling streams. The lake outlines the old system of river valleys.

What we are approaching now is the new mouth of the Whitewater. The river comes right at us, roaring out of the V of the gorge, splashing down terraces, pouring into the lake. The spectacular Lower Falls is only a short distance upstream, but if you want to see it, you have to hike in to the observation platform from the trail head at the Bad Creek Pumped Storage Station; you'd never make it from this direction. The gorge is all rushing river.

As we make our way over to the Thompson, separated from the Whitewater by the toe of that ridge I crossed on my solo hike back in December, we pass Coley and Wright Creeks on the eastern shore, both streams pouring from high shelves of stone into the lake. Nice waterfalls, but think how high they must have been before.

I'm particularly eager to scout the Thompson from this direction. Ever since the day I ate lunch on a boulder below the bridge, it has been the river I most want to fish. Come April I'm going to see if I can get Jimmy Orr to drop me at the mouth—save me the three-and-a-half mile hike in from the trailhead.

Not a chance. The mouth of the Thompson is less forbidding than the Whitewater, but it's still intimidating. A steeply slanting rock funnels the current into a narrow chute

Whitewater Falls. Nantahala National Forest, North Carolina.

through which the river comes rushing. Sally and Jane and I step from the canopied interior out onto the bow. Jimmy cuts the motor, and we go putt-putting right up to the turbulent apron of the outflow. The clear green water is rolling like seltzer, a white seethe of bubbles welling up from below. In spite of the cold, I am reminded of some blissfully refreshing drink, dreamed of on a summer afternoon. Behind us Jimmy says, "That water's pure enough to drink."

It certainly looks like it. It is so clear that I can see rocks on the bottom, 15 feet down. I can't help but wonder what else is down there—what undug sites, both aboriginal and historical, what drowned evidence of lives lived in the shadow of the wall.

To experience a place fully, I believe, one must learn something of its past, the record of human impact on that particular locale. The field of water that is Lake Jocassee not only conceals evidence, it also suppresses ghosts, but I remember enough South Carolina history to see Indians in the clear depths below. These river valleys were the domain of the Cherokee, the site of their Lower Towns, but long before the emergence of the culturally distinct tribe of that name, people were living here at the foot of the wall. Long before. While there is no evidence of Paleo hunters stalking mammoths in these hills, archaeologists have established the presence of Archaic tribesmen—hunter-gatherers who were making pottery and killing deer with spear-throwers at the same time the patriarch Abraham was driving his herds along the Jordan River. The Archaic Tradition gave way to the Woodland around the time of King David (1,000 B.C.) and the Woodland to the Mississippian in the 8th century A.D. Not until the 18th century would the native peoples living here have been recognizable as Cherokee.

At its peak, the Cherokee nation occupied the southern Appalachian region as far west as the Cumberland Plateau and south into Alabama and Georgia, but they were first encountered by English traders here in the Lower Towns of the Keowee. According to contemporary reports, the Cherokees were a tall, handsome people; they went almost naked for much of the year, lived on game and corn, and dwelt in houses made of wood and bark. Responding to the opportunity to trade deerskins for manufactured goods, they soon grew dependent on cloth, cookware, iron tools, and firearms—not to mention whiskey. As trade grew more lucrative to the English, traders became increasingly unscrupulous. Friction developed. Violence flared.

You can read the sad story of the Cherokee War in the history books. It took place in the late 1750s, and much of it was fought right here, almost within the shadow of Fort Prince George, a palisade constructed in 1753, the site of which is now covered by the waters of Lake Keowee. As wars go, there wasn't much to it—a few massacres by both sides, a couple of punitive expeditions sent out from Charles Town, and it was over. By the time of the American Revolution, former hunting grounds had been ceded to the

Crown, and the few surviving Indians had removed to lands beyond the Blue Ridge. By the turn of the century the back country of South Carolina was open to settlement.

It strikes me that this very lake provides a metaphor for the victory of white America over the Indians: as Lakes Keowee and Jocassee flood the valleys where the Lower Towns once flourished, so colonial South Carolina overwhelmed the Cherokee and obliterated their culture, saving only their lovely names.

But I see white people, too, in the clear depths below—in isolated cabins scattered up and down these valleys, poor farmers struggling to feed and clothe their families. They began to arrive in the early 19th century—Scotch-Irish people, many of whom came down the Blue Ridge from Virginia and Pennsylvania and, reaching the southern terminus, staked claims in the river valleys where Indians had planted corn a few generations before. Slowly the valleys filled. By the time of the Civil War, the Keowee was dotted with farmsteads, and cabins began to appear along the Whitewater and the Toxaway as far up as the mouths of the gorges. A few people went even further, finding in the mountains an acre level enough to plow.

They survived by growing corn and making liquor, raising hogs and cutting timber, bearing and rearing children. Tough and independent, they married among themselves, forging strong ties of blood kinship. They built schools and churches, opened stores and ran grist mills. And by the end of the century, villages had grown up around the forks of the rivers, and the upper part of Oconee County had become a vibrant rural community.

As I try to envision the hard life that flourished here 100 years ago, the meaning of the metaphor of Lake Jocassee changes. On any summer day the lake is an emblem of 20th century affluence, the American dream come true: suntanned people sailing and waterskiing, happy families in their lakefront homes, putting ribeyes on the grill, and all the while the great turbines of Jocassee generating the energy required to sustain the dream.

The mountain farmers of a century ago could not have possibly imagined the scene, but they surely dreamed of a better life—for their grandchildren if not for themselves—and often they worked themselves into early graves to bring the dream a little closer. In spite of the efforts of Duke Power to relocate graves before the dam was built, some are said to have been overlooked, forgotten then and underwater now. And those who ski and sail on Lake Jocassee—grandchildren of the children, figuratively if not literally—are too often oblivious to what lies beneath them: a boy plowing a mule through rocky ground; a man hauling corn to his still in the gorge, then moving that still by night because of the rumor of a revenuer; a woman with raw hands humming a tune in a minor key as she hangs out clothes in a cold wind; a congregation singing a capella in a plain, unpainted church; a couple burying a little girl who died of diphtheria. All that living and dying. All those stories.

I wish I had space to tell at least a few, but I can refer the reader to a book called *Keowee*, an exceptionally good local history by Michael Hembree and Dot Jackson. Well documented with the nostalgic recollections of former residents, it presents an almost idyllic image of life in the Keowee Valley, especially after the turn of the 20th century—shady lanes and covered bridges, milk cows and kitchen gardens, hotels for summer tourists and after church dinners-on-the-grounds. Accompanying photographs reveal a harsher life, especially in the faces of the subjects, but they coalesce with the verbal images to bear out the truth of a wonderful statement by an old man named Furber Whitmire: "People all lived at home. They growed their living."

Although the white settlers of the Keowee Valley ventured up into the mountains to hunt and to cut trees and to build and operate liquor stills—which fouled the streams with runoff—they probably did no more lasting damage to the land than the Indians had. Their widest roads were little more than footpaths. As late as the 1890s, give or take a few years, the Blue Ridge Escarpment was still green and wild. But the 20th century brought with it the big logging operations. They came mostly from the north, where they had leveled the forests of New England, and they bought up or leased timber rights on huge tracts of virgin land in the southern Appalachians.

It is hard for us to imagine the size of the trees—poplar, white oak, white pine, and hemlock (valuable for its bark)—that fell to the crosscut saw. It's even harder to envision a forest of such giants. The logs were so big that it often took 16 spans of oxen to move them. Some operations tried to get them out by floating them down rivers, as they had in Maine, but the fast falling streams of the Blue Ridge claimed as much timber as they moved. So the companies built narrow gauge railroads. I've been told that you can still find the road beds in the mountains above Jocassee.

Though the method of logging was not what we call clearcutting, the moving of such trees ravaged the mountainsides. Concurrent with the logging, the American chestnut blight was creeping south, destroying the predominant tree in the mountains. By the end of World War I the majestic old-growth forests of the Blue Ridge Escarpment were gone—not for good, but forever.

Much of the land along the four rivers was owned in those years by the Singer Corporation, apparently for the purpose of securing wood for sewing machines. But Duke Power, foreseeing the need for hydroelectric lakes and recognizing the Keowee Valley as a prime site, began acquiring real estate before World War II. By the early '60s, Duke was ready to draw up plans for the Keowee-Toxaway Project. In 1963 they bought 34,400 acres from Singer and from private landowners. Though many of the latter were reluctant to sell, local governments and Chambers of Commerce were thrilled by the news, and the Federal Power Commission approved a license for Duke to

Purple Ironweed and Black-Eyed Susan. Duke Power land, South Carolina.

proceed. After removing families, churches, covered bridges, and the dead, cutting valuable timber, and conducting archaeological digs—one of which discovered Fort Prince George—Duke Power began excavating. By 1973 the clear green water had backed up the channels to the mountain wall, and Lake Jocassee stood at full pond, 1,100 feet above sea level. With a shoreline of 75 miles, it covers 7,565 acres.

Our boat has entered the Horsepasture arm—a still channel at this point—but by the time we reach the wooden bridge of the Foothills Trail we are motoring against a current. Jimmy noses the pontoon into the bank just below the bridge. We hop from the bow to the bank and tie up—and find ourselves standing in a bed of Oconee bells. The plants are not in bloom, of course, but the round, leathery, copper-colored leaves are diagnostic.

On either side of the bridge the trail ascends a long, steep staircase. From here west to the Thompson, it's a seven-mile jaunt, a little further east to Laurel Fork. I want to hike the trail in both directions, but mostly I want to fish upstream. Leaning on the rail of the bridge, looking up the Horsepasture, Jimmy points out a shoal beyond which no boat can navigate. "That's wild country up there," he says.

I believe it. The river looks as though it reaches deep into the mountains, back in time as well as space, toward true wilderness. Windy Falls is up there—a couple of miles, as I recall from the map—but you'd have to wade. There are no trails along the river.

I ask Jimmy about the fishing, but the lake is his area of expertise. Just this morning I saw photographs on the walls of his store of trophy brown trout taken from Jocassee by his clients. You don't catch fish that size on an artificial fly in the river, but I prefer the challenge of reading running water and casting to it with a flyrod. I'm not very good at that, but the size of the fish is almost incidental to my purpose. I say almost because of the enormous difference between a 10-inch trout and one that goes 15—the chance of a butter-yellow brown with its beautiful spotted flanks as big as that—would keep me casting all the way to Windy Falls.

Those who once lived in the valleys now covered by the lakes went into the mountains because they had to—whether to hunt deer or to cut down trees or to make whiskey—but surely they must have found adventure in their forays and joy in the wildness of hidden coves and gorges. That experience so far has remained just beyond my reach—a little further in than I've had time to go—but sooner or later I plan to join their company.

On our way over to the Toxaway, Jimmy turns toward a secluded cove to show us the falls of Laurel Fork. There's a boat in there, a couple of fishermen casting for bass on this wet, chilly day. Jimmy cuts the motor and swings the pontoon into a slow turn so as not to make waves—the etiquette of the lake. The waterfall is a long thin cataract, white against the gloom.

The old channel of the Toxaway is Jocassee's longest arm, and the mouth, spanned by a suspension bridge—the Foothills Trail—is wide. Out of this gorge, on a late summer night in 1916, roared a wall of water that swept away everything in its path—trees, boulders, houses. Ten miles upstream the dam at Lake Toxaway—a resort for the

Cedar Creek races to join the Chauga River, a candidate for National Wild and Scenic River designation. Sumter National Forest, South Carolina.

wealthy, not unlike the present development—had given way. Miraculously, no lives were lost in the Toxaway Valley, though water backed up in the tributaries, and the Whitewater River, according to those who lived along its banks, ran backwards that night.

Those of us who love the natural world can be grateful that, given the necessity of the lake, Duke Power did it so beautifully. As I survey the forested hills from Jimmy Orr's boat, I am struck by the potential for development on the north shore—vacation homes, paved roads, maybe even a theme park—and I applaud Duke Power and its subsidiary Crescent Resources, Inc. for their commitment to protecting a wild environment. They have not undertaken this task without assistance. In partnership with resource agencies in North Carolina and South Carolina, they have established a cooperative black bear research and management program that is maintaining one of the densest populations in the southeast; they have been instrumental in the restoration of the peregrine falcon as a breeding species in South Carolina for the first time since the 1930s; in cooperation with Trout Unlimited they have improved trout habitats in streams; and with the help of the National Wild Turkey Federation they are restoring that magnificent game bird to its former mountain habitat. For such policies and programs, the National Wildlife Federation in 1985 named Duke Power recipient of its Conservation Achievement Award. The uniqueness and effectiveness of these partnerships, especially those involving the Jocassee area, have been recognized in industry magazines as a model for natural resource planning success.

Because large lakes do not occur as natural features in the South, I was unprepared to recognize the beauty of Jocassee, but that's just a prejudice. What I behold in all directions is a natural landscape with a clean, northwoods atmosphere—clear, green water, white pine and hemlock, huge boulders. It reminds me of Walden Pond or a lake in the woods of Minnesota.

We head south down the arm of the Toxaway. Jimmy calls attention to birds up ahead on the water off the starboard bow. I spot them a second before they dive—a pair of loons, winter visitors in drab winter garb, perhaps from Minnesota or descendants of the bird that laughed at Thoreau on Walden Pond. I'm glad they've found this southern lake to their liking.

And then we see the eagles. A solitary bird at first. I spot it flying low and heavy against the gray-green forest wall, white head shining, white tail flashing. As we pass, the eagle alights on the bare branch of a dead pine, right on the edge of the water, and another flies in to join it—a juvenile I judge by its uniform dark plumage.

The author wets his trout line at Three Forks where the West Fork of the Chattooga River is born. Chattahoochee National Forest, Georgia.

Swamp thistle. Caesars Head Park, Mountain Bridge Wilderness, South Carolina.

The epitome of the Blue Wall—sheer rock face of Whiteside Mountain.
Nantahala National Forest, North Carolina.

The Chattooga River flanked by ancient rock. Nantahala National Forest, North Carolina.

Miscanthus near Thompson River. Duke Power land, North Carolina.

The inexorable process of the fungus continues. Table Rock Park, Pickens County, South Carolina.

Falls of East Fork of Overlook Creek, a tributary of the West Fork of the Chattooga River.
Nantahala National Forest, North Carolina.

White cascade beside golden pool. Caesars Head Park, Mountain Bridge Wilderness, South Carolina.

Previous page: The Blue Ridge Escarpment cast in sharp relief by the setting sun.
Greenville County, South Carolina.

Jack-in-the-Pulpit and geranium flower. Sumter National Forest, South Carolina.

Icicles and small waterfall near Thompson River. Duke Power land, South Carolina.

Upper Whitewater Falls with rainbow. Nantahala National Forest, North Carolina.

Swamp Pink, a Federal Threatened Rare Species. Watson Heritage Trust Preserve, Mountain Bridge Wilderness, South Carolina.

Pattern of limbs, snow and light, along Middle Saluda River. Jones Gap Park, Mountain Bridge Wilderness, South Carolina.

THE HORSEPASTURE WATERFALLS

February 17. On the Horsepasture River with Sally Coenen. A bright, freezing morning. We pull off the highway—N.C. 281—just north of the bridge.

From here where it crosses the road, the Horsepasture begins a headlong plunge down the face of the Blue Wall—1,200 feet in two miles. Translate those figures into topography and you get a deep gorge with dramatic waterfalls. The first two—Drift and Turtleback—are right by the highway, hence the many paths down to the river. I came here with my family on a summer day seven or eight years ago, and traffic on the paths was heavy—people in swimsuits coming and going like columns of ants—and the river bank was littered with beer and soda cans. The huge boulders at the foot of Turtleback were draped with sunbathers, and you could hardly talk for the squeals of teenagers going over the falls. Drift is known locally as Bust Your Butt, or some variant of that name. It's easy to see why. Only the reckless try it. Turtleback is a less risky slide—I went down it once myself—but people have drowned in the pool at the bottom. It's called the Chug Hole.

This section along the road is the trampled fringe of a Wild and Scenic River, but on this still winter morning, temperature in the 20s, we have it to ourselves. The trash left by the summer crowds has long since been removed or washed away. The wooded banks are clean, and below us the green river sparkles in the sun.

From Bust Your Butt to Turtleback the bank of the river is braided with paths that diverge and converge and split again, as though to accommodate two-way traffic, but beyond Turtleback they funnel into one. Rainbow Falls is less than one-quarter of a mile downstream, but fewer people, it appears, make the hike.

A side trail takes us out onto open shelves of stone at the top of Rainbow. With a heavy volume of water this time of year, the river gushes over the crest in a rampage of huge white roostertails. We dare not approach the brink, but from where we stand we can see enough: the face of the gorge opposite the falls is frosted white; hemlocks are flocked like Christmas trees; and ice glazes boulders in the stream. Every surface touched by the windblown spray shines or glitters in the sun.

Back in 1984, Sally tells me, a California power company applied for federal permits to build a plant on the Horsepasture. Sally can't explain the technology they proposed, but she remembers that they talked of diverting the flow of the river from its bed into a pipeline that was to be constructed alongside. I try to imagine Rainbow without its free falling cataract, and the idea that people would willingly destroy such splendor casts a blight upon the brightness of the morning. That would have been a crime against nature if there ever was one. Local people thought so. With her father Tommy Wyche,

The Chattooga River in its younger stage. Nantahala National Forest, North Carolina.

Sally attended hearings at which residents of this area stood up and shook their unanimous fist in the face of the California dam builders. Reinforced by the efforts of a man named Bill Thomas, by Tommy Wyche and South Carolina Senator Strom Thurmond, the people succeeded in gaining the Wild and Scenic River designation for the lower four and a half miles of the Horsepasture, between here and Lake Jocassee.

A man appears on the rock shelf, a bearded guy carrying a tripod on his shoulder. We speak as he sets up his camera. From his accent I take him to be a local resident, like those fishermen I met on the Thompson. He explains that he comes here often, still looking for that perfect photograph. He's about decided, he says, to bring his video camera. "Just set it up and turn it on, let it run all day."

Sally and I are amused. Then, as we imagine the fellow in his den, watching 10 straight hours of falling water, watching the slow change of light on the constant cresting of the roostertails, we recognize the spirit that kept the carpetbaggers out.

The trail from Rainbow to Stairway shows even less evidence of use. After a mile of steady descent, it brings you to the foot of a seven-tiered waterfall. Though not as dramatic as Rainbow, Stairway acquires beauty in rough proportion to the effort we spent in getting here. The boulders at the bottom are too rounded to provide a comfortable picnic spot, but we accept the inconvenience for the sake of the view.

As we are finishing lunch, three hikers—men about my age—emerge from the wooded trail. They are on their way to Windy Falls, they say; they wonder if they are on the right path. I happen to have with me Kevin Adams' guidebook *North Carolina Waterfalls.* According to the book, Windy is less than a mile downstream, but Adams warns against that approach "unless you are a Green Beret." A safer trail, though considerably longer, branches away from the river upstream from where we are. To reach it, the hikers would have to retrace their steps, but they don't want to do that. So they dismiss the warning as hyperbole, bid us good day, and head on down the trail.

Sally is afraid they're in for a rough time. Her father has taken that trail, and he won't do it again; the warning in the guidebook means what it says. In fact, he was told by a former Green Beret who led a search for the body of a boy who drowned upstream from here that the Horsepasture Gorge is more rugged than the country he trained in. I wish the hikers no harm, but I'm glad Windy Falls, which drops 720 feet in less than a mile, is hard to reach. And even if you do, Sally says, you still can't see it all. Tommy could not find a place from which to shoot the whole waterfall. The guidebook confirms that; if you want a shot of the falls in its entirety, Adams advises, you'll have to get it from an airplane. I like knowing that: that deep in this mountain wilderness there exists a grandeur of such magnitude, whether or not I ever have a chance to try to take it in.

On the way in, Sally and I were too eager to reach our destination to spend much time at Rainbow, but on the return trip, where the trail crosses the face of the gorge opposite the falls, we stop and look up. Sally focuses her Nikon, a natural response. In the face of such extravagant beauty, even the gentlest pilgrim may feel the impulse to appropriate the experience—whether by song or dance, poetry or paint—to grab it and try to keep it. But no medium is adequate, and snapping a picture, unless you can handle a camera as Tommy does, is hardly more effective than using a glass of water to douse a forest fire.

I will try to write about this stunning white cascade, but knowing the inadequacy of words, I've already begun to despair. This causes me to wonder what I would do with Windy Falls, should I ever get there. Or would I be content just to see it, having come at last to the ultimate waterfall?

We descend from the trail, make our way down through rainbows in the mist to the ice-covered boulders at the foot. Spray wets our cheeks. I place my fingertips upon the stone-cold massive wall over which the river plunges, and I swear I feel a pulse.

Right now, like Annie Dillard, I just want to hold out my little cup and let the river fill it.

The Oconee Bell, endemic to the Blue Ridge Escarpment. Oconee County.

A water snake dries on river boulders. Chattooga River, Sumter National Forest, South Carolina.

Seed pods of a Sycamore tree become Christmas ornaments. Greenville County, South Carolina.

Nature's own sculpture, like driftwood. Caesars Head Park, Mountain Bridge Wilderness, South Carolina.

Reflections on change and permanence. Thompson River near Lake Jocassee, Duke Power land, South Carolina.

Previous page: Whiteside Mountain, the highest cliff in the East, towers over the headwaters of the Chattooga River. Nantahala National Forest, North Carolina.

More than 400 feet below the top of Upper Whitewater Falls. Nantahala National Forest, North Carolina.

Showy Orchis. Sumter National Forest, South Carolina.

A spider waits in its web on the banks of the Chauga River. Sumter National Forest, South Carolina.

A pattern of green, grey, and white on the Chattooga River. Nantahala National Forest, North Carolina.

Upper Whitewater Falls begins its plummet into the gorge. Nantahala National Forest, North Carolina.

A National Wild and Scenic River is born at Three Forks. West Fork of the Chattooga River, Chattahoochee National Forest, Georgia.

Ancient vines continue their climb to sunlight. Nantahala National Forest, North Carolina.

Horsepasture River, a national Wild and Scenic River, cloaked with snow. Duke Power land, North Carolina.

A palette of green and blue on rock. Saluda River, Pickens County, South Carolina.

A waterfall joins Oil Camp Creek. Jones Gap Park, Mountain Bridge Wilderness, South Carolina.

Previous page: Twilight scene of Table Rock Reservoir and cliffs. Table Rock Park, Pickens County, South Carolina.

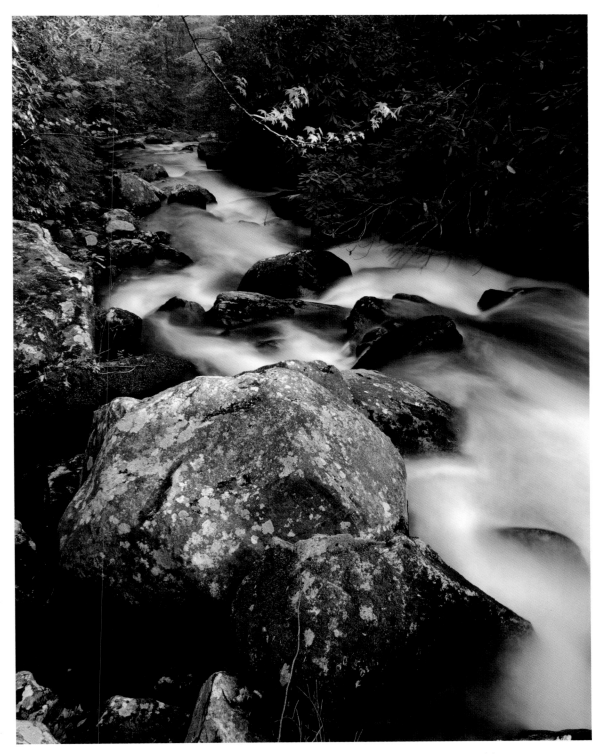

Matthews Creek cascades through a deep gorge. Caesars Head Park, Mountain Bridge Wilderness, South Carolina.

Ice sheaths vertical cliffs of Jumping Off Rock. Lake Jocassee, Duke Power land, South Carolina.

Tiger Swallowtails and Dusky Blues puddling. On the banks of the Thompson River, Duke Power land, North Carolina.

Lower Bearwallow Falls a short distance upstream from the confluence with the Toxaway River. Duke Power land, North Carolina.

An autumn vista from Jumping Off Rock. Lake Jocassee, Duke Power land, South Carolina.

71

Mushroom draws its sustenance from living tree. Table Rock Park, Pickens County, South Carolina.

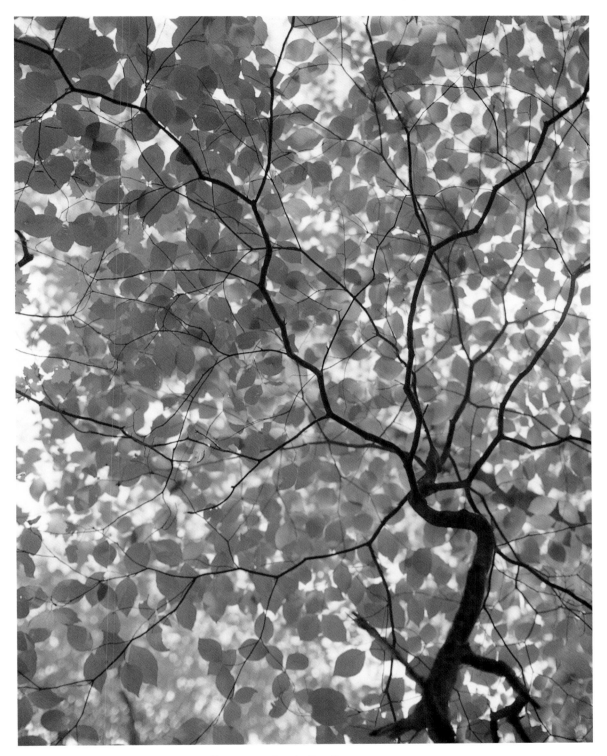

Nature's pointilism portrait. Greenville County, South Carolina.

From a Red-tail's Point of View

March 22. A helicopter lands in the Bad Creek parking lot. The pilot hops out and, stooping beneath the rotors, conducts Sally and me around the nose to doors on the other side. Sally joins her father in the cabin; I climb into the co-pilot's seat. Once we're strapped in and fitted with a headset, the craft lifts off—a slow wobble into the wind and glare.

Beneath my feet the parking lot shrinks. I see the Upper and Lower Falls on the Whitewater River, the ridge between the Whitewater and the Thompson, and a long seam that must be the Thompson River Gorge.

The chopper swings west, beating through gusts and tricky downdrafts. Turkey vultures and a lone red-tail hawk soar beneath us, sunlight glinting off their wings. We top a ridge and there's the fierce Chattooga, a silver thread among the hills. I have fished and camped and hiked down there, along Holcombe Creek and up the Chattooga to Ellicott Rock, but I never guessed that area to be so near the Jocassee gorges.

In 1813 surveyor Andrew Ellicott, who laid out the boundaries between Georgia and the two Carolinas, chiseled the date of the survey into a boulder that stands at the point where the three states meet. That boulder is right below us, surrounded by 80,000 acres of National Forest—in Georgia the Chattahoochee, the Nantahala in North Carolina and in South Carolina the Sumter—three names but one unbroken mountain woodland.

Tommy Wyche wants to photograph the Three Forks, the confluence, in Rabun County, Georgia, of Holcombe, Overflow and Big Creek that forms the West Fork of the Chattooga. The helicopter circles low, buffeted by strong gusts. The three streams converge at right angles to each other, more nearly resembling blue lines on a map than the rushing whitewater rivers they are. In fact, the whole scene looks rather tame from this point of view, the mountains reduced to gentle hills, sheer cliffs flattened. But try that country on foot. That's the only way to get into Three Forks—there are no roads—and it's not a Sunday afternoon stroll. We did it a couple of weeks ago—Tommy for the purpose of getting photographs, I simply to see an area I had been hearing about for years.

Sumac leaf.

Lower still, I spot the boulder where we ate our lunch. From there we looked upstream to the confluence—the flowing together—and beyond, on two of the streams, waterfalls.

Pictures taken, we swing back east, over the Ellicott Wilderness, and there lies Lake Jocassee, its arms reaching into the gorges, flashing like a mirror. Above it looms the dominant ridge of the Escarpment, the Blue Wall extending eastward toward Table Rock and the Mountain Bridge.

If I look to the north, I might be able to see Highlands and Cashiers and Lake Toxaway—resort communities for the affluent of Florida and Atlanta, but I don't want to destroy the illusion that the wild green country below extends from horizon to horizon. It does in fact stretch from Rabun County in Georgia to Jones Gap State Park—a 170,000-acre vestige of the original idea. Given the overheated development of the southern Appalachians during the last 20 years, most people, I expect, would be astonished to realize that a natural area of that size, with a pristine lake, spectacular waterfalls, rugged gorges, and two Wild and Scenic Rivers, still exists within a three-hour drive of a million people. If it were secured under the management of a single federal agency, it would be recognized as one of the great parks in the United States. But it's not. At the very center of the swath, directly below us now, is the keystone: the 50,000-acre Duke Power property. Though wild and rugged and virtually roadless still, its future is uncertain.

We are now above the gorge of the Horsepasture—its steep granite walls a forbidding place, even from the air, especially in this wind—and just ahead the long white tongue of Windy Falls. Kevin Adams' guidebook says that this is the only way to gain a view of the falls in its entirety, but I almost don't want to look. Seeing it from up here seems not to count. But I look anyway. The tiny shadow of the helicopter climbs the long white water. We bank into the wind and swing south. Somewhere down there, in the two miles between the foot of Windy Falls and the lake, we'll be camping tomorrow night.

The photosynthesis of spring begins. Sumter National Forest, South Carolina.

A series of falls into Lake Jocassee. Duke Power land, South Carolina.

Autumn leaves await the next rains. Saluda River, Pickens County, South Carolina.

Fern garden along small creek. Sumter National Forest, South Carolina.

Catesby's Trillium. On the banks of the Thompson River gorge, Duke Power land.

Frozen spray from Rainbow Falls. Horsepasture River, Duke Power land, North Carolina.

The morning sun peers through the fog around Whiteside Mountain. Nantahala National Forest, North Carolina.

Gentian and blackberry leaves near Thompson River. Duke Power land, South Carolina.

Previous page: Autumn colors festoon the sides of the Whitewater River gorge to Lake Jocassee. Duke Power land, North Carolina/South Carolina.

A World Champion Tulip tree (the third largest in the eastern United States). Nantahala National Forest, near Highlands, North Carolina.

Small fall over ledge. Table Rock Park, Pickens County, South Carolina.

The rock bed of the clear Whitewater River becomes burnished gold. Nantahala National Forest, North Carolina.

A still river reflects the green of the trees and blue of the sky. Table Rock Park, Pickens County, South Carolina.

Twilight and a lone boat on Lake Jocassee. Duke Power land, South Carolina.

Autumn foliage frames Chattooga River. Sumter National Forest, South Carolina.

Blackberries ready and nearly ready. Sumter National Forest, South Carolina.

IN THE HEART OF THE GORGE

March 23. This is not the way I expected it to happen. I thought that my first camping trip to the Duke Power property would be on the Thompson River, with my wife and one or more of our children or any of several trout fishing buddies, and I thought we'd backpack in. Instead, Jane and I are bringing up the rear in a caravan of three heavily loaded vehicles headed for the Horsepasture.

Compared to the vast stretches of wild country in the west, the 50,000 or 60,000 acres of the Duke Power property, or the Jocassee gorges as I have come to think of it, is a small backyard. But as I saw from the air yesterday, it is part of a much larger area, stretching west into Georgia—natural and mostly wild, extensive enough for bears and remote enough to encourage hope at least for panthers. It is also roadless, if by road you mean a public thoroughfare. We are driving in today on a rocky two-track, and we have eight miles to go before we reach our campsite on the river.

One measure of wilderness is the amount of time required to get beyond the reach of lights and traffic noise and power lines and people. Usually, that means backpacking for several hours, maybe a day or two, but here I am, at the wheel of a four-wheel drive, following two other vehicles down this steep descent. By special permission we will enjoy the luxuries of car camping. But that does mean an easy trip in. We are tilted forward at such an angle that, if it weren't for our seatbelts, we'd fall into the windshield. I'm beginning to smell my brakes. This is the face of the Wall—1,200 feet in two miles— my most breathtaking experience yet of its sudden drop.

Just when I'm thinking there's no bottom to this hill, we level out. A turn or two and there's the river—white boulders in the fast, clear green current and an open campsite beneath the pines on the bank. After that ride, it looks like home.

There are nine of us—besides Jane and me, the Wyche-Coenen connection, including Dan and Sally's two young daughters Amy and Claire. Another couple—Dave and Pam—have driven in for the day.

The agenda is to hike upstream one mile to Windy Falls, but I have come to fish.

A small holly slakes its thirst in a temporary winter pool. Caesars Head Park, Mountain Bridge Wilderness, South Carolina.

With no tent to set up, Dave is already in the river—Orvis waders, Orvis rod, fishing with a nymph. He looks as though he knows what he's doing. Just as the group sets out, Dave's rod bends. Everyone rushes to the river to watch him play the fish. It looks like a good one. It is—a rainbow, about 12 inches. I remove my own Orvis rod from its tube, joint the sections, seat the reel.

The river is wide with plenty of room for casting, and its deep, blue-green channels are strewn with boulders that create pocket water where big trout lie. My impulse to tie on an attractor fly, to watch a highly visible humpy or caddis riding lightly down the current, almost overcomes common sense. This is still March; the rainbows are spawning and feeding underwater. A friend at home advised that I use the biggest, hairiest, blackest wet fly in my collection. I choose an imitation that looks too obscene to cast on water so beautiful. Then I twist a bit of soft lead around the leader.

The bottom is treacherous, floored with rocks the size and shape of bowling balls, and the waist-deep current wants to push you off your feet. My concern with staying dry battles against a desire to get within casting distance of a deep run along the far bank. I place my feet with care, test the purchase before committing to it. I'm not confident with wet flies; I've never developed a sense of what's going on underwater. Lack of faith in the unseen, I guess.

Using a boulder for cover, I make a short cast to the deep run, strip line, try to visualize the fly bouncing along the bottom. Where the run ends I pull the fly up into the current, retrieve and cast again, feeling blind.

Keep a tight line, a voice whispers in one ear, and watch your leader. A twitch may mean a bump. Be ready.

Bam.

I've got a fish. A nice fish, hooked hard, I think. As soon as I begin to take in line, he makes a run, the rod bends, and the strength of the fish ripples like a current through the rod. I've never caught a trout this strong. Instead of playing him, I haul him gracelessly toward a rocky bar, tugging against his steady pull, lifting the rod high, wishing I had brought my landing net.

Oh, he is a nice fish—a wild rainbow, dark and striped, a spawning male.

I don't want to kill him.

Neither did Dave want to kill the one he caught. He said he'd never killed a trout in his life. But we have been challenged by scoffing non-believers to provide supper. I conk the fish on the head and slip him into the pocket on the back of my vest.

Three hours later we are sitting around a fire in the dark. Five fish, from 10 to 15 inches, feed the multitude. A third fisherman—a Greenville lawyer named Cary—contributed two. Those who scoffed now rave about fresh trout broiled over the coals of a campfire. Talk is of Windy Falls—the grueling climb straight up through dense rhododendron. Jane says she could hardly believe it when Tommy leaned out over a precipice to make a photograph, but Sally laughs and says that he's been doing that for years. Dan is excited about the Comet Hyakutake, in what constellation it's expected to appear and at what hour. He won't allow himself to believe.

It's getting nippy—temperature in the low 40s at least and still dropping. Someone puts another log on the fire, sending up a column of sparks. Sally says I must hike to Windy Falls tomorrow, but I don't commit. Not with a daylong stretch of Wild and Scenic River that hasn't been fished in a long time. The anticipation of the falls that I have lived with through the winter has been fulfilled today by my wife. If I see Windy at all it will be because I've fished my way upstream to the pool at its foot.

Dave and Pam bid us all goodnight and drive off. When I think of what they are facing in the dark, between here and the gate, I give thanks for our snug little tent a few yards away, our two down bags and the down comfort that covers them. Before turning in, I walk with Dan out to the river to look for the comet, and there it is, right on schedule, at the tail of the Big Dipper—a cold, chalky smudge in a sky as black as deep space. The hard sparkle of stars makes me shiver.

About a mile downstream from here is the Foothills Trail bridge where I stood with Jimmy Orr back in January, and he, looking toward where I am right now, said, "That's wild country up there."

With more stars in the sky tonight than most people ever see and no sound but the roar of the river in which native browns and rainbows breed, it feels wild. If not quite wild enough, that may be because of the way we came in, or the size of our party, but it occurs to me that the wilderness I seek was never geographical anyway. No matter how deep into country we go, there's always a deeper place, more remote from all points than where we are right now.

The image of that place for me is a scene painted by Winslow Homer, a print of which hangs in my living room. It is of a fisherman leaning against a huge fallen tree, playing a trout in a dark pool at the foot of a waterfall. The air is cool and misty, and the only sound is the roar of the cataract. That place lies hidden somewhere in these gorges. If ever I should stumble upon it, I would know it right away. I'll be looking for it tomorrow.

March 24. Midafternoon and I am clinging to a hickory sapling on a steep mountainside high above the Horsepasture River, utterly worn out but more fully aware than I have ever been of the topography of the gorges. Jane is 20 yards behind me, which means above my head, for we are sliding on our butts downhill, from tree to blessed tree, grabbing hold.

A full account of how we came to be here would be tedious to recite. In brief, I allowed myself this morning to be talked into what I thought would be a short hike to a waterfall on Bear Camp Creek. But the waterfall was further than I'd expected—two and a half miles, most of it straight up out of the gorge. No sooner had we arrived than Cary announced that he had to get back to Greenville for his son's birthday. Because he had left his car at the gate, 10 miles by road from where we then were, I wondered what his plan was. He was going to walk, he said. After getting as far as our camp, he planned to strike out across country; the road would take too long. I was impressed. Cary knows these mountains well; he is a veteran of the Special Forces; he knew what he was getting into. Without fanfare, he headed off. The rest of us shared lunch at the top of Bear Camp Creek Falls, and then Jane and I left Tommy and the others and started back by the Foothills Trail, which passes near the bottom.

During the three miles between the falls and the Horsepasture, a pileated woodpecker swept across the trail up ahead, two turkeys flushed from a white pine on the side of a mountain, and we paused to admire banks of *Shortia*, Oconee Bells in bloom. As lovely as the flowers were, we didn't pause for long. I was in a hurry to get back in time to fish, and the afternoon was slipping away. At 3:00 we were standing on the bridge. Camp was no more than a mile upstream; trouble was, I didn't know how to get there. We had been told that we would find fishermen's trails along the bank, but the sides of the gorge on both sides of the river rose sharply from the water. No paths there. The alternative was to follow the Foothills Trail until it met the gravel rode we'd driven in on, but who knew how long a walk that would be? We dragged ourselves up the steep staircase on the east bank and trudged on. After a while we came upon an old roadbed that forked to the left, the direction in which camp lay. I insisted that we try it.

"But what if it runs out?" Jane asked.

The truth was, I didn't care. If Cary could make it eight miles across the mountains, surely we could manage one.

"We'll just have to trust it," I said.

But it failed us, rounding a shoulder and merging into the mountain.

A cascade of pearls of falling water. Table Rock Park, Pickens County.

So here we are. Nowhere to go but down. And we are catching hold of trees as we slide toward the river. Eventually, I see large boulders through the foliage below. I assure Jane that we can't be far downstream of the camp, that we'll be able to rockhop the rest of the way.

At the river's edge I walk out onto a large flat stone and there, less than 200 yards downstream is the bridge where we were standing an hour ago.

The stones along the river take us maybe 50 yards upstream before a cliff cuts us off. I look up. The wooded mountainside is all but vertical. I can't see anything that might be taken for the top.

We climb. At every stop we gauge our strength before attempting to reach the next tree above us. Several times one or the other loses a purchase and slides back, desperate for a trunk to grab. Eager to find a way, I move out too far ahead of Jane. She calls out to me to wait. And so we come at last to the top. Through the trees above I see patches of sky. I'm hoping for the gravel road. With the remainder of my strength I pull myself up to the crest. And find myself on the spine of a narrow ridge, at the brink of a sheer drop. At least the ridge descends to the left in the direction of camp.

By going down, climbing up again, and descending once more, we come at last to floodplain, and there are the promised fishermen's paths. We stumble into camp at 5:30, take off our boots and open cans of cold beer. A few minutes later here comes Tommy's crew, exhausted from a similar ordeal on the other side. The little Coenen girls, eight and 11, appear to have survived it in good shape—an achievement that cautions me against exaggerating my own. And not a complaining word from either one the whole time, their proud father says (which is more than I can claim for myself).

No trout for supper this night, but Judy from Greenville prepares a gourmet meal on her knees in the dark. Afterwards, with greasy fingers, I light an expensive cigar and lose myself in the fire. Tommy and Sally play on harmonicas several Stephen Foster tunes. Then Sally breaks into Beethoven's "Ode to Joy." In my spirit I sing along.

March 25. What I gained in exchange for fishing yesterday is knowledge in my joints and muscles that this is vertical country. Somewhere I read that the best way to get a sense of the topography of the Jocassee Gorges is to hike the Foothills Trail from the Whitewater River to Laurel Fork. I have wanted to do that—hope to yet—but yesterday I acquired a more intimate acquaintance with this terrain than the trail can ever provide.

I remember that was Tommy's promise back in November, when first I came into this country: "Eventually we'll go down into the gorges, he said, but not until your arm is stronger; it's hand over hand."

It is indeed.

The sky is gray this morning, the weather warm. I want to get in an hour of fishing before I leave. But the rain starts sooner than any of us expected. I hardly make a cast before I feel the first drops. When I get back to camp, the site reminds me of a fire ant hill stirred by a stick. In 30 minutes we are packed and loaded up. The rain is serious now, but we're headed out, clambering up the face of the Blue Wall.

Light snow on rhododendron. Middle Saluda River, Jones Gap Park, Mountain Bridge Wilderness, South Carolina

Trees absorb the fog's moisture. Whiteside River, Nantahala National Forest, North Carolina.

Sun-drenched ferns and water. Sumter National Forest, South Carolina.

Autumn leaves, setting sun and Lake Jocassee. Duke Power land,
South Carolina.

Huge boulders are scattered throughout the Escarpment. Caesars Head Park, Mountain Bridge Wilderness, South Carolina.

Smartweed and mushrooms. Oconee Station, South Carolina.

Yellow Lady's Slipper. Sumter National Forest, South Carolina.

Glen Falls, Nantahala National Forest, near Highlands, North Carolina.

Mountain Sweet Pitcher plant, a Federal Endangered Rare Species, found in less than 40 places throughout the world. Chandler Heritage Trust Preserve, Mountain Bridge Wilderness, South Carolina.

Mountain Sweet Pitcher plant. Chandler Heritage Trust Preserve, Mountain Bridge Wilderness, South Carolina.

Windy Falls, a spectacular, long cascade hidden deep within Horsepasture River gorge. Duke Power land, North Carolina.

Previous page: Evening quiet descends on Lake Jocassee. Duke Power lands, Pickens County, South Carolina.

Foam Flower. Sumter National Forest, South Carolina.

Looking hundreds of feet down into the upper gorge of the Whitewater River. Nantahala National Forest, North Carolina.

Wake Robin Trillium. Sumter National Forest, South Carolina.

The Toxaway River, flanked by steep mountain sides, will soon join Lake Jocassee.
Duke Power land, North Carolina.

Shadbush. Sumter National Forest, South Carolina.

AFTERWORD

THE GIFT OF WILD PLACES

Thirty years ago a young tourist traveling west from North Carolina received the same thrill as millions before him and millions after: that first glimpse of tops of snow-laden peaks of the Rocky Mountains rising behind the Great Plains. It was an indelible moment. Eight years later and three days after college graduation, I was headed west again, sorry to be leaving my beloved North Carolina, but excited to be seeking prosperity in Colorado. Though I found no sizeable fortune, I fell in love with the American West, and for almost twenty years have made my living by recording the beauty of nature on film.

I, like Tommy Wyche, have hiked many miles in search of nature's sublime offerings. I have explored some of the most remote wilderness in the continental United States, and witnessed sights and sounds and experienced moments unique to any I could have ever imagined. From mountains and plains to canyons and coast, I have discovered places that are bastions of ecological health and diversity, as valuable as any on our planet.

For me, our wildest places are our best places. Wilderness is an unequalled stabilizing force that is always there and connects us with our beginnings. The personal sense of security derived from things permanent, like wilderness and God, is more important now than ever before as the world becomes more crowded and chaotic. And yet, wilderness is not a static landscape frozen in time,

Lower Whitewater Falls, one of the highest waterfalls in the Blue Ridge Escarpment. Duke Power land, South Carolina.

of any natural place are our vision, our wisdom, and our will to keep pristine wilderness lands to excite and inspire the generations that follow.

I often tell the story about the time my son, J.T., accidentally put an ice pick through his finger. It was a Saturday morning, I was just about to leave on a photography excursion. As always, I was excited to be heading into the wilds for a week of creativity and therapy with nature. A lengthy stay in the emergency room of the hospital unfortunately caused the postponement of my trip. Sitting in the waiting room, feeling sorry for my son and a bit sorry for myself, I reflected on the value of wild places.

I couldn't help thinking that the physical act of being in wilderness might not actually be as important as the mere knowledge it exists. Yes, we derive great pleasure by recreating in nature in so many ways. We certainly need the solitude of wild places and open spaces to soothe our minds following a week of city noises. And where else can one better learn about natural systems and the web of life that sustains us all? Yet, the act of going there may be insignificant when compared to simply knowing that there is such a place to retreat from the pressures of human society. Whether sitting in front of a computer terminal in a high-rise office or standing in a factory line looking

but a living, dynamic environment full of the fury and calm of nature. To explore vast wildernesses, we must abandon worldly schedules and immerse ourselves in the flows and patterns of nature—rise with the sun, sleep with the darkness, huddle from the storm.

In today's age of nuclear catastrophes, oil spills, and destruction of earth's ozone layer, perhaps we should ask ourselves some serious questions about the degree to which we live in harmony with the natural world. Toward what end are we taking our civilization if we do not arrest our disrespect for the environment? The defining factors

forward to that weekend hike along a mountain trail, isn't the realization that we have the ability to "get away from it all" at least as valuable as doing it? The psychological boost that we gain from knowing that wild places exist comforts the soul and lends us a sense of security not available from any other worldly source.

The Blue Wall is such a wild place. May it always be there in total naturalness, for the sake of the web of life, as well as for those of us who cannot survive without it.

—John Fielder
Englewood, Colorado